THE KNOPF POETRY SERIES

The Dead and the Living is the 1983
Lamont Poetry Selection of the
Academy of American Poets.

From 1954 through 1974 the Lamont
Poetry Selection supported the
publication and distribution of
twenty first books of poems. Since
1975 this distinguished award has
been given for an American poet's
second book.

Judges for 1983: June Jordan,
Charles Simic, and David Wagoner

The Dead
and the Living

The Dead
and the Living

Poems by
Sharon Olds

Alfred A. Knopf   New York   1995

THIS IS A BORZOI BOOK
PUBLISHED BY ALFRED A. KNOPF, INC.

Copyright © 1975, 1978, 1979, 1980, 1981, 1982, 1983 by Sharon Olds

All rights reserved under International and Pan-American Copyright
Conventions. Published in the United States by Alfred A. Knopf, Inc.,
New York, and simultaneously in Canada by Random House of Canada
Limited, Toronto. Distributed by Random House, Inc., New York.

Most of the poems in this collection have appeared in the following
publications: *Alcatraz, The Atlantic, Cincinnati Poetry Review, Contact/II,
Iowa Review, Kayak, The Massachusetts Review, Michigan Quarterly Review,
New England Review, The New Republic, New York Quarterly Review,
Open Places, Ploughshares, The Poetry Miscellany, Poetry Northwest,
Poets On, Prairie Schooner, A Shout in the Street, Tar River Poetry,
The Yale Review.*

"Photograph of the Girl" originally appeared in *The Missouri Review.*
"Things That Are Worse Than Death" and "The Eye" originally appeared
in *The Nation.* Copyright 1982 Nation Magazine, The Nation Associates, Inc.
"The Winter After Your Death" originally appeared in *The New Yorker.*
"Ideographs," "The Guild," "The Fear of Oneself," "Armor" and "Burn
Center" were first published in *Poetry.* "Pre-Adolescent in Spring" was first
published in *The Seattle Review.*

Library of Congress Cataloging in Publication Data

Olds, Sharon. The dead and the living.
  I. Title. II. Series.
PS3565.L34D4 1983   811'.54   83-47780
ISBN 0-394-53048-9
    0-394-71563-2

I wish to thank the John Simon Guggenheim Memorial Foundation
and the National Endowment for the Arts for their generous support
during the completion of this book.

Manufactured in the United States of America
Published February 21, 1984
Reprinted Fourteen Times
Sixteenth Printing, September 1995

For George and Mary Oppen

Contents

Part One

Poems for the Dead

I. Public

Ideographs

(*a photograph of China, 1905*)

The small scaffolds, boards in the form of
ideographs, the size of a person,
lean against a steep wall of
dressed stone. One is the simple
shape of a man. The man on it
is asleep, his arms nailed to the wood.
No timber is wasted; his fingertips
curl in at the very end of the plank
as a child's hands open in sleep.
The other man is awake—he looks
directly at us. He is fixed to a more
complex scaffold, a diagonal cross-piece
pointing one arm up, one down,
and his legs are bent, the spikes through his ankles
holding them up off the ground,
his knees cocked, the folds of his robe flowing
sideways as if he were suspended in the air
in flight, his naked leg bared.
They are awaiting execution, tilted against the wall
as you'd prop up a tool until you needed it.
They'll be shouldered up over the crowd and
carried through the screaming. The sleeper will wake.
The twisted one will fly above the faces, his
garment rippling.
Here there is still the backstage quiet,
the dark at the bottom of the wall, the props
leaning in the grainy half-dusk.
He looks at us in the silence. He says
Save me, there is still time.

Photograph of the Girl

The girl sits on the hard ground,
the dry pan of Russia, in the drought
of 1921, stunned,
eyes closed, mouth open,
raw hot wind blowing
sand in her face. Hunger and puberty are
taking her together. She leans on a sack,
layers of clothes fluttering in the heat,
the new radius of her arm curved.
She cannot be not beautiful, but she is
starving. Each day she grows thinner, and her bones
grow longer, porous. The caption says
she is going to starve to death that winter
with millions of others. Deep in her body
the ovaries let out her first eggs,
golden as drops of grain.

Race Riot, Tulsa, 1921

The blazing white shirts of the white men
are blanks on the page, looking at them is like
looking at the sun, you could go blind.
Under the snouts of the machine guns,
the dark glowing skin of the women and
men going to jail. You can look at the
gleaming horse-chestnuts of their faces the whole day.
All but one descend from the wood
back of the flat-bed truck. He lies,
shoes pointed North and South,
knuckles curled under on the splintered slats,
head thrown back as if he is in a
field, his face tilted up
toward the sky, to get the sun on it, to
darken it more and more toward the color of the human.

Portrait of a Child

*(Yerevan, capital of a republic
set up by those Armenians who had
not been massacred by the Turks.
In 1921, Turkey and Russia
divided the republic between them.)*

His face is quite peaceful, really,
like any child asleep, though the skin
is darkened in places, the curved eyelids
turgid, part of the ear missing
as if bitten off. He lies like a child
asleep, on his side, one arm bent
so the hand curls near his face, one arm
dangling across his chest, fingertips
touching the stone street. His shirt has
two rents near the waist, the slits hunters make
in the stomach of the catch.
Besides the shirt he wears nothing. His abdomen is
swollen as the belly of a pregnant woman
and sags to one side. His hip-joint bulges,
a bruise. His thigh is big around as a
newborn's arm, and from hip-bone to knee
the tendon runs sharp as a crease in cloth,
the skin pulling at it. His knees are enormous,
his feet peaceful as in deep sleep,
and across one leg delicately rests
his penis. Pale and lovely there
at the center of the picture, it lies, the source
of the children he would have had, this child
dead of hunger
in Yerevan.

Nevsky Prospekt

(July 1917)

It is an old photo, very black and
very white. One woman
lifts up her heavy skirt as she runs.
A man in a white jacket, his hands
tied behind his back, runs,
his chin stuck out. An old woman
in massive black turns and looks behind her.
A man throws himself onto the pavement.
A child in heavy boots is running
but looks back over his shoulder
at the black and white heap of bodies.
The wide grey stone square
is dotted with fallen inky shapes
and dropped white hats. Everything else is
heaving away like a sea from the noise we
feel in the silence of the photograph
the way the deaf see sound: the terrible
voice of the submachine guns saying
This is more important than your life.

The Death of Marilyn Monroe

The ambulance men touched her cold
body, lifted it, heavy as iron,
onto the stretcher, tried to close the
mouth, closed the eyes, tied the
arms to the sides, moved a caught
strand of hair, as if it mattered,
saw the shape of her breasts, flattened by
gravity, under the sheet,
carried her, as if it were she,
down the steps.

These men were never the same. They went out
afterwards, as they always did,
for a drink or two, but they could not meet
each other's eyes.

Their lives took
a turn—one had nightmares, strange
pains, impotence, depression. One did not
like his work, his wife looked
different, his kids. Even death
seemed different to him—a place where she
would be waiting,

and one found himself standing at night
in the doorway to a room of sleep, listening to a
woman breathing, just an ordinary
woman
breathing.

The Issues

(Rhodesia, 1978)

Just don't tell me about the issues.
I can see the pale spider-belly head of the
newborn who lies on the lawn, the web of
veins at the surface of her scalp, her skin
grey and gleaming, the clean line of the
bayonet down the center of her chest.
I see her mother's face, beaten and
beaten into the shape of a plant,
a cactus with grey spines and broad
dark maroon blooms.
I see her arm stretched out across her baby,
wrist resting, heavily, still, across the
tiny ribs.
             Don't speak to me about
politics. I've got eyes, man.

Aesthetics of the Shah

*(The poster, up all over town, shows
dissidents about to be executed in Iran)*

The first thing you notice
is the skill
used on the ropes, the narrow close-grained
hemp against that black cloth
the bodies are wrapped in. You can see the fine
twist-lines of the twine, dark and
elegant, the intervals exact,
and the delicate loops securing the bagged
bodies to the planks like cradle boards.
The heads are uncovered, just the eyes
bound with rag. Underneath
the mustaches like blood. There is not a
white hair on the whole row,
not a strand. They are young men and
still alive, swaddled to the neck in this
black bunting, the ropes lovely as
spider-lines against wet stone.

Things That Are Worse Than Death

(for Margaret Randall)

You are speaking of Chile,
of the woman who was arrested
with her husband and their five-year-old son.
You tell how the guards tortured the woman, the man, the child,
in front of each other,
"as they like to do."
Things that are worse than death.
I can see myself taking my son's ash-blond hair in my fingers,
tilting back his head before he knows what is happening,
slitting his throat, slitting my own throat
to save us that. Things that are worse than death:
this now idea enters my life.
The guard enters my life, the sewage of his body,
"as they like to do." The eyes of the five-year-old boy, Dago,
watching them with his mother. The eyes of his mother
watching them with Dago. And in my living room as a child,
the word, Dago. And nothing I experienced was worse than death,
life was beautiful as our blood on the stone floor
to save us that—my son's eyes on me,
my eyes on my son—the ram-boar on our bodies
making us look at our old enemy and bow in welcome,
gracious and eternal death
who permits departure.

II. Private

The Guild

Every night, as my grandfather sat
in the darkened room in front of the fire,
the liquor like fire in his hand, his eye
glittering meaninglessly in the light
from the flames, his glass eye baleful and stony,
a young man sat with him
in silence and darkness, a college boy with
white skin, unlined, a narrow
beautiful face, a broad domed
forehead, and eyes amber as the resin from
trees too young to be cut yet.
This was his son, who sat, an apprentice,
night after night, his glass of coals
next to the old man's glass of coals,
and he drank when the old man drank, and he learned
the craft of oblivion—that young man
not yet cruel, his hair dark as the
soil that feeds the tree's roots,
that son who would come to be in his turn
better at this than the teacher, the apprentice
who would pass his master in cruelty and oblivion,
drinking steadily by the flames in the blackness,
that young man my father.

Grandmother Love Poem

Late in her life, when we fell in love,
I'd take her out from the nursing home
for a chaser and two bourbons. She'd crack
a joke sharp as a tin lid
hot from the teeth of the can-opener,
and cackle her crack-corn laugh. Next to her
wit, she prided herself on her hair,
snowy and abundant. She would lift it up
at the nape of the neck, there in the bar,
and under the white, under the salt-and-
pepper, she'd show me her true color,
the color it was when she was a bride:
like her sex in the smoky light she would show me
the pure black.

The Eye

My bad grandfather wouldn't feed us.
He turned the lights out when we tried to read.
He sat alone in the invisible room
in front of the hearth, and drank. He died
when I was seven, and Grandma had never once
taken anyone's side against him,
the firelight on his red cold face
reflecting extra on his glass eye.
Today I thought about that glass eye,
and how at night in the big double bed
he slept facing his wife, and how the limp
hole, where his eye had been, was open
towards her on the pillow, and how I am
one-fourth him, a brutal man with a
hole for an eye, and one-fourth her,
a woman who protected no one. I am their
sex, too, their son, their bed, and
under their bed the trap-door to the
cellar, with its barrels of fresh apples, and
somewhere in me too is the path
down to the creek gleaming in the dark, a
way out of there.

Birthday Poem for My Grandmother

(for L.B.M.C., 1890–1975)

I stood on the porch tonight— which way do we
face to talk to the dead? I thought of the
new rose, and went out over the
grey lawn— things really
have no color at night. I descended
the stone steps, as if to the place where one
speaks to the dead. The rose stood
half-uncurled, glowing white in the
black air. Later I remembered
your birthday. You would have been ninety and getting
roses from me. Are the dead there
if we do not speak to them? When I came to see you
you were always sitting quietly in the chair,
not knitting, because of the arthritis,
not reading, because of the blindness,
just sitting. I never knew how you
did it or what you were thinking. Now I
sometimes sit on the porch, waiting,
trying to feel you there like the color of the
flowers in the dark.

Of All the Dead That Have Come
to Me, This Once

I have never written against the dead. I would
       open my
shirt to them and say yes, the white
cones still making sugary milk,

but when Grandfather's gold pocketwatch
came in by air over the Rockies,
over the dark yellow of the fields
and the black rivers, with Grandmother's blank
face pressed against his name in the back,

I thought of how he put the empty
plate in front of my sister, turned out
the lights after supper, sat in the black
room with the fire, the light of the flames
flashing in his glass eye
in that cabin where he taught my father
how to do what he did to me, and I said

No. I said Let this one be dead.
Let the fall he made through that glass roof,
splintering, turning, the great shanks and
slices of glass in the air, be his last
appearance here.

Farewell Poem

(for M. M. O., 1880–1974)

The big, cut iceberg waits
outside the harbor like a spaceship.
Sends in emissaries: cold
chopped fish, floating cakes,
canoes of ice white as brides.
Lurks just beyond the warm
furred lip of the harbor, summer
berries in the bushes, loud stink
of fish drying on salty wooden
slats. Waits. Hides nine
tenths of its iron implacable
bulk under the belt of the water,
frigid as cods' teeth, even
now in July. The sea bathes
her endless pale scarred hips.
The berg sits, cute as a hat,
snowy as egret feathers, waiting
to call the next one out to the other
world beyond the absolutely
frozen vessel.

        She walks down
to the water without her walker.
With none of her three canes she was always
losing, joking about, looking for,
finding over her arm. She just
had her hair done, silver curls
obedient as ivy tendrils
over her child's brow. She wears
the grey dress with a white collar,
sensible shoes, white socks,

diamond pin, sets her foot
on the cloudy crystal of an ice floe
and floats out to her mother, floats
out to the white iceberg waiting
ninety-three years for hot death
to deliver his favorite daughter home to
the cool white long room,
lace curtains from the parlor flying
like flags in the summer sky.

The Winter After Your Death

(*for Katie Sheldon Brennan*)

The long bands of mellow light
across the snow
narrow slowly.
The sun closes her gold fan
and nothing is left but black and white—
the quick steam of my breath, the dead
accurate shapes of the weeds, still, as if
pressed in an album.
Deep in my body my green heart
turns, and thinks of you. Deep in the
pond, under the thick trap
door of ice, the water moves,
the carp hangs like a sun, its scarlet
heart visible in its side.

Miscarriage

When I was a month pregnant, the great
clots of blood appeared in the pale
green swaying water of the toilet.
Dark red like black in the salty
translucent brine, like forms of life
appearing, jelly-fish with the clear-cut
shapes of fungi.

That was the only appearance made by that
child, the dark, scalloped shapes
falling slowly. A month later
our son was conceived, and I never went back
to mourn the one who came as far as the
sill with its information: that we could
botch something, you and I. All wrapped in
purple it floated away, like a messenger
put to death for bearing bad news.

The End

We decided to have the abortion, became
killers together. The period that came
changed nothing. They were dead, that young couple
who had been for life.
As we talked of it in bed, the crash
was not a surprise. We went to the window,
looked at the crushed cars and the gleaming
curved shears of glass as if we had
done it. Cops pulled the bodies out
bloody as births from the small, smoking
aperture of the door, laid them
on the hill, covered them with blankets that soaked
through. Blood
began to pour
down my legs into my slippers. I stood
where I was until they shot the bound
form into the black hole
of the ambulance and stood the other one
up, a bandage covering its head,
stained where the eyes had been.
The next morning I had to kneel
an hour on that floor, to clean up my blood,
rubbing with wet cloths at those dark
translucent spots, as one has to soak
a long time to deglaze the pan
when the feast is over.

Best Friends

(for Elizabeth Ewer, 1942-51)

The day my daughter turned ten, I thought of the
lank, glittering, greenish cap of your
gold hair. The last week of
your life, when I came each day after school,
I'd study the path to your front door,
the bricks laid close as your hairs. I'd try to
read the pattern, frowning down
for a sign.
       The last day—there was not
a mark on that walk, not a stone out of place—
the nurses would not let me in.

We were nine. We had never mentioned death
or growing up. I had no more imagined
you dead
than you imagined me
a mother. But when I had a daughter
I named her for you, as if pulling you back
through a crack between the bricks.
       She is ten now, Liddy.
She has outlived you, her dark hair gleaming like
the earth into which the path was pressed,
the path to you.

Absent One

(for Muriel Rukeyser)

People keep seeing you and telling me
how white you are, how thin you are.
I have not seen you for a year, but slowly you are
forming above my head, white as
petals, white as milk, the dark
narrow stems of your ankles and wrists,
until you are always with me, a flowering
branch suspended over my life.

Part Two

Poems for the Living

I. The Family

Possessed

(for my parents)

I have never left. Your bodies are before me
at all times, in the dark I see
the stars of your teeth in their fixed patterns
wheeling over my bed, and the darkness
is your hair, the fragrance of your two heads
over my crib, your body-hairs
which I count as God counts the feathers of the sparrows,
one by one. And I never leave your sight,
I can look in the eyes of any stranger and
find you there, in the rich swimming
bottom-of-the-barrel brown, or in the
blue that reflects from the knife's blade,
and I smell you always, the dead cigars and
Chanel in the mink, and I can hear you coming,
the slow stopped bear tread and the
quick fox, her nails on the ice,
and I dream the inner parts of your bodies, the
coils of your bowels like smoke, your hearts
opening like jaws, drops from your glands
clinging to my walls like pearls in the night.
You think I left—I was the child
who got away, thousands of miles,
but not a day goes past that I am not
turning someone into you.
Never having had you, I cannot let you go, I
turn now, in the fear of this moment,
into your soft stained paw
resting on her breast, into your breast trying to
creep away from under his palm—
your gooseflesh like the shells of a thousand tiny snails,
your palm like a streambed gone dry in summer.

The Victims

When Mother divorced you, we were glad. She took it and
took it, in silence, all those years and then
kicked you out, suddenly, and her
kids loved it. Then you were fired, and we
grinned inside, the way people grinned when
Nixon's helicopter lifted off the South
Lawn for the last time. We were tickled
to think of your office taken away,
your secretaries taken away,
your lunches with three double bourbons,
your pencils, your reams of paper. Would they take your
suits back, too, those dark
carcasses hung in your closet, and the black
noses of your shoes with their large pores?
She had taught us to take it, to hate you and take it
until we pricked with her for your
annihilation, Father. Now I
pass the bums in doorways, the white
slugs of their bodies gleaming through slits in their
suits of compressed silt, the stained
flippers of their hands, the underwater
fire of their eyes, ships gone down with the
lanterns lit, and I wonder who took it and
took it from them in silence until they had
given it all away and had nothing
left but this.

The Forms

I always had the feeling my mother would
die for us, jump into a fire
to pull us out, her hair burning like
a halo, jump into water, her white
body going down and turning slowly,
the astronaut whose hose is cut
falling
      into
            blackness. She would have
covered us with her body, thrust her
breasts between our chests and the knife,
slipped us into her coat pocket
outside the showers. In disaster, an animal
mother, she would have died for us,

but in life as it was
she had to put herself
first.
She had to do whatever he
told her to do to the children, she had to
protect herself. In war, she would have
died for us, I tell you she would,
and I know: I am a student of war,
of gas ovens, smothering, knives,
drowning, burning, all the forms
in which I have experienced her love.

The Departure

(to my father)

Did you weep like the Shah when you left? Did you forget
the way you had had me tied to a chair, as
he forgot the ones strapped to the grille
in his name? You knew us no more than he knew them,
his lowest subjects, his servants, and we were
silent before you like that, bowing
backwards, not speaking, not eating unless we were
told to eat, the glass jammed to our
teeth and tilted like a brass funnel in the
soundproof cells of Teheran. Did you forget
the blood, blinding lights, pounding on the door, as
he forgot the wire, the goad,
the stone table? Did you weep as you left
as Reza Pahlevi wept when he rose
over the gold plain of Iran, did you
suddenly want to hear our voices, did you
start to rethink the darkness of our hair,
did you wonder if perhaps we had deserved to live,
did you love us, then?

Burn Center

When my mother talks about the Burn Center
she's given to the local hospital
my hair lifts and wavers like smoke
in the air around my head. She speaks of the
beds in her name, the suspension baths and
square miles of lint, and I think of the
years with her, as her child, as if
without skin, walking around scalded
raw, first degree burns over ninety
percent of my body. I would stick to doorways I
tried to walk through, stick to chairs as I
tried to rise, pieces of my flesh
tearing off easily as
well-done pork, and no one gave me
a strip of gauze, or a pat of butter to
melt on my crackling side, but when I would
cry out she would hold me to her
hot griddle, when my scorched head stank she would
draw me deeper into the burning
room of her life. So when she talks about her
Burn Center, I think of a child
who will come there, float in water
murky as tears, dangle suspended in a
tub of ointment, suck ice while they
put out all the tiny subsidiary
flames in her hair near the brain, and I say
Let her sleep as long as it takes, let her walk out
without a scar, without a single mark to
honor the power of fire.

The Ideal Father

When I dream you, Dad, you come into the dream
clean, *farouche*, *gesundheit*, feral
fresh face, physically exact—
the ideal, the schemata, the blueprint, no mark of
pain. You're perfect as a textbook example:
your hair like a definition of hair,
the bulb with its pith which contains a little air,
the root, the spear of horny substance, the
mouth of the follicle, the filament which forms the
coat of the mammal, the way the sheath
glistens where the shaft opens its oil to the light;
and your skin, the layers of the epidermis like
clear water through which we see the
subcutaneous fat, its pearls
swimming in cross-section; and your teeth, their
pork-white ceilings, enamel crowns,
pulp hollows, necks and roots like
squids' legs, deep in the gum—not a
cavity, no whiff of rot; and your
body flawless, pink carnation
boutonnières of the nipples; and your sex
stiffening in textbook time,
record time, everything about you
exemplary. Where is the one who threw up?
The one who passed out, the one who would not
speak for a week, slapped the glasses off a
small girl's face, bloodied his head and

sank through the water? I think he is dead.
I think the ideal father would hardly
let such a man live. After all he has
daughters to protect, laying his perfect
body over their sleep all night long.

Fate

Finally I just gave up and became my father,
his greased, defeated face shining toward
anyone I looked at, his mud-brown eyes
in my face, glistening like wet ground that
things you love have fallen onto
and been lost for good. I stopped trying
not to have his bad breath,
his slumped posture of failure, his sad
sex dangling on his thigh, his stomach
swollen and empty. I gave in
to my true self, I faced the world
through his sour mash, his stained acrid
vision, I floated out on his tears.
I saw the whole world shining
with the ecstasy of his grief, and I
myself, he, I, shined,
my oiled porous cheeks glaucous
as tulips, the rich smear of the petal,
the bulb hidden in the dark soil,
stuck, impacted, sure of its rightful place.

My Father Snoring

Deep in the night, I would hear it through the wall—
my father snoring, the great, dark
clotted mucus rising in his nose and
falling, like coils of seaweed a wave
brings in and takes back. The clogged roar
filled the house. Even down in the kitchen,
in the drawers, the knives and forks hummed with that
distant throbbing. But in my room
next to theirs, it was so loud
I could feel myself inside his body,
lifted on the knotted rope of his life
and lowered again, into the narrow
dark well, its amber walls
slick around my torso, the smell of bourbon
rich as sputum. He lay like a felled
beast all night and sounded his thick
buried stoppered call, like a cry for
help. And no one ever came:
there were none of his kind around there anywhere.

The Moment

When I saw the dark Egyptian stain,
I went down into the house to find you, Mother—
past the grandfather clock, with its huge
ochre moon, past the burnt
sienna woodwork, rubbed and glazed.
I went deeper and deeper down into the
body of the house, down below the
level of the earth. It must have been
the maid's day off, for I found you there
where I had never found you, by the wash tubs,
your hands thrust deep in soapy water,
and above your head, the blazing windows
at the surface of the ground.
You looked up from the iron sink,
a small haggard pretty woman
of 40, one week divorced.
"I've got my period, Mom," I said,
and saw your face abruptly break open and
glow with joy. "Baby," you said,
coming toward me, hands out and
covered with tiny delicate bubbles like seeds.

My Father's Breasts

Their soft surface, the polished silk of the hair
running down them delicately like
water. I placed my cheek—once,
perhaps—upon their firm shape,
my ear pressed against the black
charge of the heart within. At most
once—yet when I think of my father
I think of his breasts, my head resting
on his fragrant chest, as if I had spent
hours, years, in that smell of black pepper and
turned earth.

The Takers

Hitler entered Paris the way my
sister entered my room at night,
sat astride me, squeezed me with her knees,
held her thumbnails to the skin of my wrists and
peed on me, knowing Mother would
never believe my story. It was very
silent, her dim face above me
gleaming in the shadows, the dark gold
smell of her urine spreading through the room, its
heat boiling on my legs, my small
pelvis wet. When the hissing stopped, when the
hole had been scorched in my body, I lay
crisp and charred with shame and felt her
skin glitter in the air, her dark
gold pleasure unfold as he stood over
Napoleon's tomb and murmured *This is the
finest moment of my life.*

The Pact

We played dolls in that house where Father staggered with the
Thanksgiving knife, where Mother wept at
noon into her one ounce of
cottage cheese, praying for the strength not to
kill herself. We kneeled over the
rubber bodies, gave them baths
carefully, scrubbed their little
orange hands, wrapped them up tight,
said goodnight, never spoke of the
woman like a gaping wound
weeping on the stairs, the man like a stuck
buffalo, baffled, stunned, dragging
arrows in his hide. As if we had made a
pact of silence and safety, we kneeled and
dressed those tiny torsos with their elegant
belly-buttons and minuscule holes
high on the buttock to pee through, and all that
darkness in their open mouths, so that I
have not been able to forgive you for giving your
daughter away, letting her go at
eight as if you took Molly Ann or
Tiny Tears and held her head
under the water in the bathinette
until no bubbles rose, or threw her
dark rosy body on the fire that
burned in that house where you and I
barely survived, sister, where we
swore to be protectors.

The Derelict

He passes me on the street, his hair
matted, skin polished with grime,
muttering, suit stained and stiffened—
and yet he is so young, his blond beard like a
sign of beauty and power. But his hands,
strangely flat, as if nerveless, hang and
flap slightly as he walks, like hands of
someone who has had polio, hands
that cannot be used. I smell the waste of his
piss, I see the ingot of his beard,
and think of my younger brother, his beauty,
coinage and voltage of his beard, his life
he is not using, like a violinist whose
hands have been crushed so he cannot play—
I who was there at the crushing of his hands
and helped to crush them.

Late Speech with My Brother

I can see you now so vividly,
fine head tilted back,
bold Teutonic jaw stiff, the
bristle along it glistens and your blue
eyes glitter like glass. I have always
feared you would take your life, I have seen you
taking your life for thirty-five years,
taking it cell by cell. I can see you
throw away your body as easily
as you thrust your whole thumb that time
into the moving machinery, so
gracefully, as if you understood
the union of science and the human. I can see you
sending your body to hell as they sent us to
bed without supper, you're as big as them now
and as proud, you would die before you would break and say
Please, don't. Please, don't
do their work for them,
don't produce a stopped life like some
work of art, the bottle fallen
away from your open hand. It is not
too late, your life is ahead of you,
behind you is your thirty-five years of
death—I have seen a man of eighty
drop his parents' hands and just walk the other way.

The Elder Sister

When I look at my elder sister now
I think how she had to go first, down through the
birth canal, to force her way
head-first through the tiny channel,
the pressure of Mother's muscles on her brain,
the tight walls scraping her skin.
Her face is still narrow from it, the long
hollow cheeks of a Crusader on a tomb,
and her inky eyes have the look of someone who has
been in prison a long time and
knows they can send her back. I look at her
body and think how her breasts were the first to
rise, slowly, like swans on a pond.
By the time mine came along, they were just
two more birds in the flock, and when the hair
rose on the white mound of her flesh, like
threads of water out of the ground, it was the
first time, but when mine came
they knew about it. I used to think
only in terms of her harshness, sitting and
pissing on me in bed, but now I
see I had her before me always
like a shield. I look at her wrinkles, her clenched
jaws, her frown-lines—I see they are
the dents on my shield, the blows that did not reach me.
She protected me, not as a mother
protects a child, with love, but as a
hostage protects the one who makes her
escape as I made my escape, with my sister's
body held in front of me.

II. The Men

The Connoisseuse of Slugs

When I was a connoisseuse of slugs
I would part the ivy leaves, and look for the
naked jelly of those gold bodies,
translucent strangers glistening along the
stones, slowly, their gelatinous bodies
at my mercy. Made mostly of water, they would shrivel
to nothing if they were sprinkled with salt,
but I was not interested in that. What I liked
was to draw aside the ivy, breathe the
odor of the wall, and stand there in silence
until the slug forgot I was there
and sent its antennae up out of its
head, the glimmering umber horns
rising like telescopes, until finally the
sensitive knobs would pop out the ends,
delicate and intimate. Years later,
when I first saw a naked man,
I gasped with pleasure to see that quiet
mystery reenacted, the slow
elegant being coming out of hiding and
gleaming in the dark air, eager and so
trusting you could weep.

Poem to My First Lover

Now that I understand, I like to
think of your terror—handed a girl
mad with love, her long, fresh
raw body thin as a pared
soap, breasts round and high and
opalescent as bubbles of soap,
laid across your legs, 18,
untouched. I like to understand your
terror, now, the way you took her,
deflowering her as you'd gut a fish,
leaving in the morning with talk of a wife.
     Now that I
know about the fear of love
I like to think of her white-hot body
greenish as a fish just landed, quivering and
slapping on a rock—fallen into your
lap, man, shuddering like your cock,
a woman crazed with love, hot off the
press, sharp as a tool never used,
blazing across your thighs and all you could
do in your fear was firk out her cherry like an
escargot from its dark shell and then
toss her away. I am in awe of terror that will
waste so much, I am in love with the girl who went
offering, came to you and
laid it out like a feast on a platter, the
delicate flesh—yes, yes,
I accept the gift.

New Mother

A week after our child was born,
you cornered me in the spare room
and we sank down on the bed.
You kissed me and kissed me, my milk undid its
burning slip-knot through my nipples,
soaking my shirt. All week I had smelled of milk,
fresh milk, sour. I began to throb:
my sex had been torn easily as cloth by the
crown of her head, I'd been cut with a knife and
sewn, the stitches pulling at my skin—
and the first time you're broken, you don't know
you'll be healed again, better than before.
I lay in fear and blood and milk
while you kissed and kissed me, your lips hot and swollen
as a teen-age boy's, your sex dry and big,
all of you so tender, you hung over me,
over the nest of the stitches, over the
splitting and tearing, with the patience of someone who
finds a wounded animal in the woods
and stays with it, not leaving its side
until it is whole, until it can run again.

The Line

When we understood it might be cancer,
I lay down beside you in the night,
my palm resting in the groove of your chest,
the rachis of a leaf. There was no question of
making love: deep inside my body that
small hard lump. In the half-light
of my half-life, my hand in the beautiful
sharp cleft of your chest, the valley of the
shadow of death,
there was only the present moment, and as you
slept in the quiet, I watched you as one watches
a newborn child, aware each moment of the
miracle, the line that has been crossed
out of the darkness.

The Fear of Oneself

As we get near the house, taking off our gloves,
the air forming a fine casing of
ice around each hand,
you say you believe I would hold up under torture
for the sake of our children. You say you think I have
courage. I lean against the door and weep,
the tears freezing on my cheeks with brittle
clicking sounds.
I think of the women standing naked
on the frozen river, the guards pouring
buckets of water over their bodies till they
glisten like trees in an ice storm.

I have never thought I could take it, not even
for the children. It is all I have wanted to do,
to stand between them and pain. But I come from a
long line
of women
who put themselves
first. I lean against the huge carved
cold door, my face glittering with
glare ice like a dangerous road,
and think about hot pokers, and goads,
and the skin of my children, the delicate, tight,
thin top layer of it
covering their whole bodies, softly
glimmering.

Poem to My Husband from
My Father's Daughter

I have always admired your courage. As I see you
embracing me, in the mirror, I see I am
my father as a woman, I see you bravely
embrace him in me, putting your life in his
hands as mine. You know who I am—you can
see his hair springing from my head like
oil from the ground, you can see his eyes,
reddish as liquor left in a shot-glass and
dried dark, looking out of my face,
and his firm sucking lips, and the breasts
rising frail as blisters from his chest,
tipped with apple-pink. You are fearless, you
enter him as a woman, my sex like a
wound in his body, you flood your seed in his
life as me, you entrust your children to that
man as a mother, his hands as my hands
cupped around their tiny heads. I have never
known a man with your courage, coming
naked into the cage with the lion, I
lay my enormous paws on your scalp I
take my great tongue and begin to
run the rasp delicately
along your skin, humming: as you enter
ecstasy, the hairs lifting
all over your body, I have never seen a
happier man.

Sex Without Love

How do they do it, the ones who make love
without love? Beautiful as dancers,
gliding over each other like ice-skaters
over the ice, fingers hooked
inside each other's bodies, faces
red as steak, wine, wet as the
children at birth whose mothers are going to
give them away. How do they come to the
come to the   come to the   God   come to the
still waters, and not love
the one who came there with them, light
rising slowly as steam off their joined
skin? These are the true religious,
the purists, the pros, the ones who will not
accept a false Messiah, love the
priest instead of the God. They do not
mistake the lover for their own pleasure,
they are like great runners: they know they are alone
with the road surface, the cold, the wind,
the fit of their shoes, their over-all cardio-
vascular health—just factors, like the partner
in the bed, and not the truth, which is the
single body alone in the universe
against its own best time.

Ecstasy

As we made love for the third day,
cloudy and dark, as we did not stop
but went into it and into it and
did not hesitate and did not hold back we
rose through the air, until we were up above
timber line. The lake lay
icy and silver, the surface shirred,
reflecting nothing. The black rocks
lifted around it into the grainy
sepia air, the patches of snow
brilliant white, and even though we
did not know where we were, we could not
speak the language, we could hardly see, we
did not stop, rising with the black
rocks to the black hills, the black
mountains rising from the hills. Resting
on the crest of the mountains, one huge
cloud with scalloped edges of blazing
evening light, we did not turn back,
we stayed with it, even though we were
far beyond what we knew, we rose
into the grain of the cloud, even though we were
frightened, the air hollow, even though
nothing grew there, even though it is a
place from which no one has ever come back.

III. The Children

Exclusive

(for my daughter)

I lie on the beach, watching you
as you lie on the beach, memorizing you
against the time when you will not be with me:
your empurpled lips, swollen in the sun
and smooth as the inner lips of a shell;
your biscuit-gold skin, glazed and
faintly pitted, like the surface of a biscuit;
the serious knotted twine of your hair.
I have loved you instead of anyone else,
loved you as a way of loving no one else,
every separate grain of your body
building the god, as I built you within me,
a scaled world. What if from your lips
I had learned the love of other lips,
from your starred, gummed lashes the love of
other lashes, from your shut, quivering
eyes the love of other eyes,
from your body the bodies,
from your life the lives?
Today I see it is there to be learned from you:
to love what I do not own.

Six-Year-Old Boy

We get to the country late at night
in late May, the darkness is warm and
smells of half-opened lilac.
Our son is asleep on the back seat,
his wiry limbs limp and supple
except where his hard-on lifts his pajamas like the
earth above the shoot of a bulb.
I say his name, he opens one eye and it
rolls back to the starry white.
I tell him he can do last pee
on the grass, and he smiles on the surface of sleep like
light on the surface of water.
He pulls his pajamas down and there it
is, gleaming like lilac in the dark,
hard as a heavy-duty canvas fire-hose
shooting its steel stream.
He leans back, his pale face
blissful. The piss, lacy and fragile,
arcs over the black lawn.
Afterwards, no hands,
he shakes himself dry, cock tossing like a
horse's white neck, and then he
leans against the car, grinning,
eyes closed, sound asleep,
his sex pointing straight ahead,
leading him
as if by the nose
into his life, late May,
June, late June, July,
full summer.

Eggs

My daughter has turned against eggs. Age six
to nine, she cooked them herself, getting up
at six to crack the shells, slide the
three yolks into the bowl,
slit them with the whisk, beat them till they hissed
and watch the pan like an incubator as they
firmed, gold. Lately she's gone from
three to two to one and now she
cries she wants to quit eggs.
It gets on her hands, it's slimy, and it's hard
to get all the little things out:
puddles of gluten glisten on the counter
with small, curled shapes floating in their
sexual smear. She moans. It is getting
too close. Next birthday she's ten and then
it's open season, no telling when
the bright, crimson dot appears
like the sign on a fertilized yolk. She has carried
all her eggs in the two baskets
woven into her fine side,
but soon they'll be slipping down gently,
sliding. She grips the counter where the raw
whites jump, and the spiral shapes
signal from the glittering gelatine, and she
wails for her life.

Size and Sheer Will

The fine, green pajama cotton,
washed so often it is paper-thin and
iridescent, has split like a sheath
and the glossy white naked bulbs of
our son's toes thrust forth like crocus
this early Spring. The boy is growing
as fast as he can, elongated
wrists dangling, lean meat
showing between the shirt and the belt.
If there were a rack to stretch himself, he would
strap his slight body to it.
If there were a machine to enter,
skip the next ten years and be
sixteen immediately, this boy would
do it. All day long he cranes his
neck, like a plant in the dark with a single
light above it, or a sailor under
tons of green water, longing
for the surface, for his rightful life.

For My Daughter

That night will come. Somewhere someone will be
entering you, his body riding
under your white body, dividing
your blood from your skin, your dark, liquid
eyes open or closed, the slipping
silken hair of your head fine
as water poured at night, the delicate
threads between your legs curled
like stitches broken. The center of your body
will tear open, as a woman will rip the
seam of her skirt so she can run. It will happen,
and when it happens I will be right here
in bed with your father, as when you learned to read
you would go off and read in your room
as I read in mine, versions of the story
that changes in the telling, the story of the river.

Rite of Passage

As the guests arrive at my son's party
they gather in the living room—
short men, men in first grade
with smooth jaws and chins.
Hands in pockets, they stand around
jostling, jockeying for place, small fights
breaking out and calming. One says to another
How old are you? Six. I'm seven. So?
They eye each other, seeing themselves
tiny in the other's pupils. They clear their
throats a lot, a room of small bankers,
they fold their arms and frown. *I could beat you
up*, a seven says to a six,
the dark cake, round and heavy as a
turret, behind them on the table. My son,
freckles like specks of nutmeg on his cheeks,
chest narrow as the balsa keel of a
model boat, long hands
cool and thin as the day they guided him
out of me, speaks up as a host
for the sake of the group.
We could easily kill a two-year-old,
he says in his clear voice. The other
men agree, they clear their throats
like Generals, they relax and get down to
playing war, celebrating my son's life.

Relinquishment

On a black night in early March,
the fire hot, my daughter says
Wrap me in something. I get the old
grey quilt, gleaming like a sloughed
insect casing, and wrap it around and
around her narrow nine-year-old body,
hollow and flexible. *Cover my face,*
she hisses in excitement. I cover her face
and fall back from the narrow, silver
shape on the carpet.
                    How finally
she is getting away—an Egyptian child
bound in gauze, set in a boat
on a black night in early March
and pushed out on the water, given
over to the gods of the next world
who will find her
or not find her.

Son

Coming home from the women-only bar,
I go into my son's room.
He sleeps—fine, freckled face
thrown back, the scarlet lining of his mouth
shadowy and fragrant, his small teeth
glowing dull and milky in the dark,
opal eyelids quivering
like insect wings, his hands closed
in the middle of the night.

                    Let there be enough
room for this life: the head, lips,
throat, wrists, hips, penis,
knees, feet. Let no part go
unpraised. Into any new world we enter, let us
take this man.

Pre-Adolescent in Spring

Through the glass door thin as a light freeze on the pond,
my girl calls me out.
She is sucking ice, a cup of cubes
beside her, sparkling and loosening.
The sun glints in her hair dark as the
packed floor of the pine forest,
its hot resin smell rising like a
smell of sex. She leaps off the porch and
runs on the grass, her buttocks like an unripe
apricot. She comes back, hair
smoking, face cool and liquid,
skin that vital, translucent white of the
casing of milk-weed pods. She fishes
another cube from the cup with her tongue.
Around us the flat spears of bulbs
are rising from inside the ground.
Above us the buds are opening. I hold
tight to this child beside me, and she
leans her body against me, heavy,
its layers still folded, its fragrance only
half unlocked, but the ice now rapidly
melting in her mouth.

Blue Son

All day with my blue son,
sick again, the blue skin
under his eyes, blue tracing of his
veins over the bones of his chest
pronounced as the ribs of the dead, a green
vein in his groin, blue-green as the
numbers on an arm. His eloquent face
grows thinner each hour, the germs use him
like a soap. Exhaustion strips him, and under each
layer of sweetness a deeper layer of
sweetness is bared. His white skin,
so fine it has no grain, goes blue-
grey, and the burning blue of his eye
dies down and goes out, it is the faded cobalt on the
side of a dead bird. He seems to
withdraw to a great distance, as if he is
gone and looking back at me
without regret, patient, like an old
man who has just dug his grave and
waits at the edge, in the evening light,
naked, blue with cold, in terrible
obedience.

Pajamas

My daughter's pajamas lie on the floor
inside out, thin and wrinkled as
peeled skins of peaches when you ease the
whole skin off at once.
You can see where her waist emerged, and her legs,
her arms, and head, the fine material
gathered in rumples like skin the caterpillar
ramped out of and left to shrivel.
You can see, there at the center of the bottoms,
the raised cotton seam like the line
down the center of fruit, where the skin first splits
and curls back. You can almost see the hard
halves of her young buttocks, the precise
stem-mark of her sex. Her shed
skin shines at my feet, and in the air there is a
sharp fragrance like peach brandy—
the birth-room pungence of her released life.

The Killer

Whenever there's a lull in the action, my son
sights along his invisible sights and
picks things off. He eyes a pillar
three rows over, pivots and easily
fires—a hit, you can tell by the flames and
smoke reflected in his glittering eyes.
Everything becomes a target—
cops topple, a whole populace
falls as he aims, yet I know this boy,
kind and tender. He whirls and lets them
have it. Tangents straighter than the arc of his
pee connect him to all he sees
like a way to touch: as the spider travels its
silver wires, our son goes out along his
line of fire, marking each thing
with the sign of his small ecstatic life.

The Sign of Saturn

Sometimes my daughter looks at me with an
amber black look, like my father
about to pass out from disgust, and I remember
she was born under the sign of Saturn,
the father who ate his children. Sometimes
the dark, silent back of her head
reminds me of him unconscious on the couch
every night, his face turned away.
Sometimes I hear her talking to her brother
with that coldness that passed for reason in him,
that anger hardened by will, and when she rages
into her room, and slams the door,
I can see his vast blank back
when he passed out to get away from us
and lay while the bourbon turned, in his brain,
to coal. Sometimes I see that coal
ignite in her eyes. As I talk to her,
trying to persuade her toward the human, her little
clear face tilts as if she can
not hear me, as if she were listening
to the blood in her own ear, instead,
her grandfather's voice.

Armor

Just about at the triple-barreled pistol
I can't go on. I sink down
as if shot, beside the ball of its butt
larded with mother-of-pearl. My son
leaves me on the bench, and goes on. Hand on
hip, he gazes at a suit of armor,
blue eyes running over the silver,
looking for a slit. He shakes his head,
hair greenish as the gold velvet
cod-skirt hanging before him in volutes
at a metal groin. Next, I see him
facing a case of shields, fingering
the sweater over his heart, and then
for a long time I don't see him, as a mother will
lose her son in war. I sit
and think about men. Finally the boy
comes back, sated, so fattened with gore
his eyelids bulge. We exit under the
huge tumescent jousting irons,
their pennants a faded rose, like the mist
before his eyes. He slips his hand
lightly in mine, and says *Not one of those
suits is really safe.* But when we
get to the wide museum steps
railed with gold like the descent from heaven,
he can't resist,
and before my eyes, down the stairs,
over and over, clutching his delicate
unprotected chest, my son
dies, and dies.

35/10

Brushing out my daughter's dark
silken hair before the mirror
I see the grey gleaming on my head,
the silver-haired servant behind her. Why is it
just as we begin to go
they begin to arrive, the fold in my neck
clarifying as the fine bones of her
hips sharpen? As my skin shows
its dry pitting, she opens like a small
pale flower on the tip of a cactus;
as my last chances to bear a child
are falling through my body, the duds among them,
her full purse of eggs, round and
firm as hard-boiled yolks, is about
to snap its clasp. I brush her tangled
fragrant hair at bedtime. It's an old
story—the oldest we have on our planet—
the story of replacement.

The Missing Boy

(for Etan Patz)

Every time we take the bus
my son sees the picture of the missing boy.
He looks at it like a mirror—the dark
blond hair, the pale skin,
the blue eyes, the electric-blue sneakers with
slashes of jagged gold. But of course that
kid is little, only six and a half,
an age when things can happen to you,
when you're not really safe, and our son is seven,
practically fully grown—why, he would
tower over that kid if they could
find him and bring him right here on this bus and
stand them together. He sways in the silence
wishing for that, the tape on the picture
gleaming over his head, beginning to
melt at the center and curl at the edges as it
ages. At night, when I put him to bed,
my son holds my hand tight
and says he's sure that kid's all right,
nothing to worry about, he just
hopes he's getting the food he likes,
not just any old food, but the food
he likes the most, the food he is used to.

Bread

When my daughter makes bread, a cloud of flour
hangs in the air like pollen. She sifts and
sifts again, the salt and sugar
close as the grain of her skin. She heats the
water to body temperature
with the sausage lard, fragrant as her scalp
the day before hair-wash, and works them together on a
floured board. Her broad palms
bend the paste toward her and the heel of her hand
presses it away, until the dough
begins to snap, glossy and elastic as the
torso bending over it,
this ten-year-old girl, random specks of
yeast in her flesh beginning to heat,
her volume doubling every month now, but still
raw and hard. She slaps the dough and it
crackles under her palm, sleek and
ferocious and still leashed, like her body, no
breasts rising like bubbles of air toward the
surface of the loaf. She greases the pan, she is
shaped, glazed, and at any moment goes
into the oven, to turn to that porous
warm substance, and then under the
knife to be sliced for the having, the tasting, and the
giving of life.

Bestiary

Nostrils flared, ears pricked,
our son asks me if people can mate with
animals. I say it hardly
ever happens. He frowns, fur and
skin and hooves and slits and pricks and
teeth and tails whirling in his brain.
You *could* do it, he says, not wanting the
world to be closed to him in any
form. We talk about elephants
and parakeets, until we are rolling on the
floor, laughing like hyenas. Too late,
I remember love—I backtrack
and try to slip it in, but that is
not what he means. Seven years old,
he is into hydraulics, pulleys, doors which
fly open in the side of the body,
entrances, exits. Flushed, panting,
hot for physics, he thinks about lynxes,
eagles, pythons, mosquitos, girls,
casting a glittering eye of use
over creation, wanting to know
exactly how the world was made to receive him.

The One Girl at the Boys' Party

When I take our girl to the swimming party
I set her down among the boys. They tower and
bristle, she stands there smooth and sleek,
her math scores unfolding in the air around her.
They will strip to their suits, her body hard and
indivisible as a prime number,
they'll plunge in the deep end, she'll subtract
her height from ten feet, divide it into
hundreds of gallons of water, the numbers
bouncing in her mind like molecules of chlorine
in the bright blue pool. When they climb out,
her ponytail will hang its pencil lead
down her back, her narrow silk suit
with hamburgers and french fries printed on it
will glisten in the brilliant air, and they will
see her sweet face, solemn and
sealed, a factor of one, and she will
see their eyes, two each,
their legs, two each, and the curves of their sexes,
one each, and in her head she'll be doing her
wild multiplying, as the drops
sparkle and fall to the power of a thousand from her body.

The Couple

On the way to the country, they fall asleep
in the back seat, those enemies,
rulers of separate countries, sister and
brother. Her big hard head
lolls near his narrow oval skull
until they are crown to crown, brown
hair mingling like velvet. Mouths
open, the rosebud and her cupid's bow,
they dream against each other, her calm
almond eyes and his round blue eyes
closed, quivering like trout. Their toes
touching opposite doors, their hands in
loose fists, their heads together in
unconsciousness, they look like a small
royal bride and groom, the bride still a
head taller, married as children
in the Middle Ages, for purposes of state,
fighting all day, and finding their only
union in sleep, in the dark solitary
power of the dream—the dream of ruling the world.

Sharon Olds was born in San Francisco and educated at
Stanford University and Columbia University. She has been
the recipient of a National Endowment for the Arts grant and
a Guggenheim Foundation Fellowship, and her poems have
appeared in *The New Yorker*, *Poetry*, *The Atlantic Monthly*,
The Paris Review, and *The Nation*. Her first book of
poems, *Satan Says*, was published in 1980 and received the
inaugural San Francisco Poetry Center Award. She lives in
New York City.

This book was set on the Linotype in Janson, a recutting
made direct from type cast from matrices long thought to have
been made by the Dutchman Anton Janson, who was a
practicing type founder in Leipzig during the years 1668–1687.
However, it has been conclusively demonstrated that these types
are actually the work of Nicholas Kis (1650–1702), a
Hungarian, who most probably learned his trade from the
master Dutch type founder Dirk Voskens. The type is
an excellent example of the influential and sturdy Dutch types
that prevailed in England up to the time William Caslon
developed his own incomparable designs from them.

Composed, printed, and bound by Heritage Printers, Inc.,
Charlotte, North Carolina

Designed by Judith Henry